About This Book

Title: *Sloths*

Step: 3

Word Count: 162

Skills in Focus: Digraph th

Tricky Words: live, trees, vines, rainforest, covers, claws, upside, ground, baby, leaves, fur

Ideas For Using This Book

Before Reading:
- **Comprehension:** Look at the title and cover image together. Ask readers what they know about sloths. What new things do they think they might learn in this book?
- **Accuracy:** Practice saying the tricky words listed on page 1.
- **Phonics and Phonemic Awareness:** Have readers look at the book's title. Help them blend the sounds they see in the word *sloths*. Bring attention to the *th* in the word. Explain that this is a digraph, two letters that make one sound when they are together. Ask readers to say the word in the title again and help them tap out the sounds in the word. Emphasize the /th/ sound and say it louder as you tap. Ask readers to watch and listen for other *th* examples in the text.

During Reading:
- Have readers point under each word as they read it.
- **Decoding:** If readers are stuck on a word, help them say each sound and blend the sounds together smoothly. Be sure to point out any words with /th/ sounds.
- **Comprehension:** Invite students to talk about what new things they are learning about sloths while reading. What are they learning that they didn't know before?

After Reading:
Discuss the book. Some ideas for questions:
- Have you ever seen a sloth? What did you notice about what the sloth looked like?
- What do you still wonder about sloths?

Sloths

Text by Laura Stickney

Reading Consultant
Deborah MacPhee, PhD
Professor, School of Teaching and Learning
Illinois State University

PICTURE WINDOW BOOKS
a capstone imprint

Sloths live in the tops of tall, thick trees.

Sloths hang on vines in the lush rainforest.

Sloths have long arms.
Thick fur covers a sloth's skin.

Bugs such as moths and ticks live on a sloth's fur.

Sloths do not move fast. But sloths are strong. Sloths can have 2 or 3 long, thick claws.

The sloth can grip and clasp a branch with its claws. Both claws help the sloth hang upside down.

Sloths can slash and clutch things with their claws.

Sloths munch on things such as twigs, leaves, and buds. Crunch!

Sloths can get to the ground.

Then they dig with their claws. They swim. Splash!

Sloths can have babies.

A baby sloth is born with thin fur.

The sloth clings to its mom's thick fur.

The baby sloth clings to the mom for months.

Both sloths swing from branch to branch. They munch on things.

Sloths can do lots of things! What do you think of sloths?

More Ideas:

Phonics and Phonemic Awareness Activity

Practicing Digraph *th*:
Write the story words *thin*, *then*, and *with*. Have readers tap out the sounds down their arm, starting at their shoulders. Ask readers how many sounds they hear in the word. Remind them that the *t* and *h* make one sound when they are together, even though they are two letters. Continue with words that have more than three sounds, such as *sloth*, *moths*, and *things*.

Extended Learning Activity

Sloth Habitat:
Ask readers to think about where a sloth might live and what it might eat. Have them draw a picture of a sloth in its habitat. Then ask readers to write three sentences about the sloth and its habitat. Challenge students to include words with /th/ sounds in their sentences.

Published by Picture Window Books, an imprint of Capstone
1710 Roe Crest Drive, North Mankato, Minnesota 56003
capstonepub.com

Copyright © 2026 by Capstone.
All rights reserved. No part of this publication may be reproduced in whole or in part, or stored in a retrieval system, or transmitted in any form or by any means, electronic, mechanical, photocopying, recording, or otherwise, without written permission of the publisher.

Library of Congress Cataloging-in-Publication Data is available on the Library of Congress website.

ISBN: 9798875227073 (hardback)
ISBN: 9798875230080 (paperback)
ISBN: 9798875230066 (eBook PDF)

Image Credits: iStock: Damocean, 7, efenzi, 4, 13, webguzs, 10-11; Shutterstock: Damsea, cover, Elfred Tseng, 14, Enrico Pescantini, 8-9, imageBROKER.com, 6, Joseph Dube-Arsenault, 20-21, Manamana, 18-19, Mark_Kostich, 17, Martijn Smeets, 15, Milan Zygmunt, 1, 2-3, 16, 22-23, 24, mrs.hizzle, 5, zampe238, 12

Printed and bound in China. 6274